Contents

1914: The Coming of the First World War

*This pamphlet argues that the outbreak of the First World War
represented not so much the culmination of a long process started
by Bismarck and his successors, as the relatively sudden breakdown
of a system that had in fact preserved the peace and contained the
dangerous Eastern Question for over a generation. It examines the
implications for all the Great Powers of the upheaval that destroyed
the balance in South-East Europe after 1912, threatened to destroy
the balance in Europe altogether and led the Great Powers into war
in the summer of 1914. It also analyses the factors — diplomatic,
military, economic, social and domestic-political — that lay behind
the decisions of that fateful summer.*

The European States System and the Eastern Question

In the summer of 1914 the Great
Powers of Europe went to war with
each other for the first time in forty
years; and this 'First World War' was
the first conflict to involve all the
European Great Powers for exactly a
hundred years. The question arises as
to why the long peace came to an end
when it did. After all, the century that
followed the defeat of Napoleon had
been one of remarkable order and
stability as far as the Great Powers
were concerned. It is true that its
middle decades had seen a series of
limited wars that had resulted in the
drastic re-ordering of the post-
Napoleonic settlement in central
Europe, with the creation of the
kingdom of Italy in 1861 and of the

German Empire ten years later. But since 1871 the continent of Europe had been divided between a group of five indisputably 'Great' Powers of roughly equal status, none of whom had any territorial designs against another that were likely to lead to war. France, it is true, could never accept that Alsace and Lorraine were lost for ever; but no other Power was prepared to support her in launching a war to recover the provinces, and there was no question of her attempting alone to reverse the verdict of 1871. For the rest, the Great Powers of Europe were all content to live within the territorial settlement of 1871; and both the network of defensive alliances built up since 1879, and the military superiority of Germany, her allies, and associates, tended to reinforce the status quo. It seemed that the days were past when a Great Power, like the France of Louis XIV or the two Napoleons, or the Prussia of Frederick the Great or even of Bismarck in his younger years, were ready to resort to war to bring about major alterations in the balance of power.

Even so, the territorial order of 1871 and the Great Power system based upon it, were fatally flawed. The Ottoman Empire had not been stabilised or incorporated into the European states system, either in 1815 or in 1871. It was Europe's Achilles' heel. Not that the 'Eastern Question' was really a problem created by the Great Powers and their clashing ambitions. It was, rather, something that had arisen to confront the Powers, a reflection of the simple fact that the Ottoman Empire was increasingly threatened with disintegration in an age when nationalism was developing amongst its subject peoples. The statesmen of Europe were, moreover,

perfectly aware of the danger inherent in the Eastern Question — of the fact that the disintegration of the Ottoman Empire would create a power vacuum in the Near East, with far-reaching implications for the stability of the balance within the European states system itself. It was for this very reason that they devoted so much of their energy to an effort to manage the Eastern Question by diplomacy, and to defer the collapse of the Ottoman Empire as long as possible. The great Eastern crisis of the 1870s, which marked a major stage in the retreat of Turkey from Europe, with the creation of a series of independent and semi-independent states in the Balkans, served to remind the Powers of the dangerous conflict of interests in the area. It was not until 1912, however, that the Eastern Question began to get really out of control, and that the fatal weakness in the European states system threatened to destroy the whole structure which had kept the peace for over forty years.

For many decades south-east Europe had in fact posed a potential threat to the vital interests of Austria-Hungary. The Habsburg Monarchy, an agglomeration of territories inhabited by some eleven nationalities, owed its existence as a Great Power to the dynastic principle and an international system based on respect for treaty rights. Its interests were, therefore, directly challenged by the principle of nationality, which asserted that state boundaries should be drawn along national lines. It was self interest as much as legitimist high principle that determined the Austrians in 1866 'not to acknowledge the principle of nationalities...We are determined to take our position in defence of our principles and our rights, which are based on treaties'. This attitude remained fundamental to Austro-Hungarian foreign policy down to 1914. It had already led the Monarchy, in 1859 and 1866, into wars against stronger Great Powers that had ended in its expulsion from Italy and Germany. Austria-Hungary was understandably sensitive, therefore, when a threat arose in the only remaining area in which it could assert itself as a Great Power, the South East. There, in 1878, the Congress of Berlin had created independent states such as Serbia and Rumania, which might be tempted some day to advance irredentist claims against not only Ottoman but also Habsburg territory — half the South Slav and Rumanian populations of Europe lived inside the Habsburg Empire. Obviously, these states posed in themselves less of a threat to the Empire than had the France of Napoleon III or the Prussia of Bismarck. Indeed, a mere threat of war — against Rumania in 1882 and against Serbia in 1909 — was sufficient to put a damper on irredentist outbursts that were too loud to ignore; and the Monarchy was for long periods able to rely on its economic and dynastic influence to restrain the Balkan kingdoms. But the danger remained that if ever a Great Power sought to encourage nationalism in the Balkans to establish its own influence in the area, threatening the integrity of the Habsburg Monarchy in the south, Vienna would resort to war yet a third time.

Only Russia might pose such a challenge. Although the commercial expansion of Great Britain, France, and Germany in the Near East tended to undermine Austria-Hungary's economic influence there and strengthen the self-confidence of the Balkan states, none of these Powers was inclined to encourage their disruptive territorial ambitions; and Italy, although a rival of Austria-Hungary for influence on the east coast of the Adriatic, was at one with her in opposing Serbian expansion there. In Russia, however, there were powerful currents of opinion — in the army, the bureaucracy, the diplomatic corps and the intelligentsia — which were strongly attached to the idea of Russia's mission to protect, if not to determine, the future of the Slav peoples beyond her borders; and who dreamed of liberating the Slavs of both Turkey and Austria-Hungary. As the Panslav general R.A. Fadayev declared in a sensational book in 1870, 'the road to Constantinople lies through Vienna'.

This is not to say, however, that the imperial Russian government — 'official Russia' — was the creature of such pressure groups. Ever since the Crimean War Russian emperors had been acutely fearful of a conflict with a modern Great Power. Alexander II had taken great care, before going to war with Turkey in 1877, to assure the Austrians that he had no intention of launching a revolutionary Slav crusade. 'Official Russia' was above all concerned for the security of the Straits at Constantinople. The Straits were Russia's economic lifeline — the gateway through which the grain exports of southern Russia passed to the west. These grain exports were vital for the development of Russian industry, and for the servicing of the foreign loans on which depended her whole economic and military development — indeed, her very existence as a Great Power. The brief closure of the Straits for even a couple of weeks in 1912, during the Italo-Ottoman war, had caused an enormous financial crisis in Russia: her agricultural exports for the first six months of 1912 were 45 per cent down on those for the corresponding six months of 1911.[1] Hence the Russian government's concern to establish its influence over the area that lay between the Central Powers and Constantinople — perhaps by establishing some sort of Balkan League under Russian auspices. But if this was essentially a defensive policy, it also had the effect of linking the Russian government's objectives to those of the 'unofficial' Russia; and these were regarded, in Austria-Hungary at least, as offensive in the extreme.

It was the quest for security, the driving force of the foreign policies of both Russia and Austria-Hungary, that was to lead those two Powers on to a collision course and to drag Europe into war in 1914. The more the Austrians tried to control the Balkan states and Turkey, the more desperate the Russians became to establish their own kind of Balkan League. What seemed defensive at St Petersburg appeared in Vienna to threaten the Dual Monarchy. It was indeed this fact, that the clash of Russian and Austro-Hungarian interests in the Near East was essentially a clash of two defensive strategies, that made the problem so dangerous and so intractable. Had it been a clash of two expansionist imperialisms on the offensive it would have been easier to manage: the Habsburgs had survived the collapse of their colonial and Mediterranean ambitions in the eighteenth century; and Russia was able to withdraw from her Far Eastern adventures after 1905 without endangering her security. But in the Near East, neither Power believed it could allow the other to attain complete security without fatally jeopardising its own security. If the question were ever posed point blank, it could be resolved only by force; and this was the issue in 1914.

The Eastern Question contained, 1878-1912: the crisis, 1912-1914

Until 1914, however, the question was not so posed. The underlying conflict had been apparent since the Congress of Berlin, or even the Crimean War; yet it was peacefully contained for over two generations. The 1914 crisis may indeed be seen not so much in terms of a positive drive to war on the part of the belligerents as of the breakdown of a system that had given Europe half a century of peace. In other words, in the generation before 1914 certain factors were operating, and certain options were available, to enable statesmen to contain even quite serious crises by diplomatic meanoeuvring. By about 1913, however, these restraining factors that facilitated compromise were ceasing to operate; and governments which had managed to co-exist peacefully for over a generation became determined on a military solution.

The Ottoman Empire, for example, constituted, until its almost total disappearance from Europe in 1912-13, an important stabilising element in the European states system. Despite its deficiencies, and the successive crises caused by its inability to satisfy its Christian subjects, the Empire functioned as a shock-absorber in the international system. It acted as a buffer between the Great Powers, for whose conflicting interests it provided a safeguard, perhaps not ideal for any, but tolerable for all. Within the confines of this inert and labyrinthine power structure, there was room for all the Powers to manoeuvre, and for all to maintain a measure of influence. No Power was confronted with the choice between sacrificing all its influence, even vital interests, and war; and, after decades of manoeuvring, the Powers and the Turks had achieved a measure of understanding of each others' ways. The participants knew, and generally respected, the rules of the game. On the one hand, the Turks had too much experience and guile, and too strong an instinct for self-preservation, ever to throw in their lot with one Power to an extent that would threaten the vital interests of another. On the other hand, the Powers had developed the habit of making compromises to cover up conflicts of interests which, if stated in extreme terms, would admit of no solution. It was not least to the Empire of 'Abdul the Damned' that Europe owed half a century of peace in the Eastern question. By the same token, when the Ottoman Empire in Europe disappeared, with astonishing rapidity, in the autumn of 1912, to be replaced by a number of small, unstable, expansionist states, it is perhaps no accident that European war followed in a little over a year.

Both Vienna and St Petersburg had long been aware of the underlying clash of interests in the Near East, and of their common interest in co-operating to maintain the Ottoman Empire as a stabilising element. They were also acutely aware — and the Paris Commune of 1871 had served as an awful reminder — of the disasters that might overwhelm the ruling elites of both empires if peaceful co-existence should fail. 'There is in Europe a great revolutionary subversive party,' the Austro-Hungarian ambassador in St Petersburg declared in 1885, 'just waiting for the crash, and for the great conservative Powers to weaken and exhaust each other in...conflict, and then the radical reform can begin.' With such considerations in mind, the two governments managed to establish, for the greater part of the half-century before 1914, a tolerable working relationship. These prolonged periods of Austro-Russian co-operation — the Three Emperors' League of 1873-78, the Three Emperors' Alliance of 1881-87, and the Austro-Russian Entente of 1897-1908 — were all based on two principles: monarchical solidarity against the Revolution, and the renunciation of attempts to disturb the status quo in the Near East. It was notable, however, that Austro-Russian co-operation always came to an abrupt end — in 1878, 1887, and 1908 — whenever one partner decided that the other was manoeuvring to secure its own predominance in the area; and that it then always took some years — more than a decade after the crisis of 1887, for example — before the aggrieved party recovered its faith sufficiently to embark on a further round of co-operation. It is possible that Austro-Russian relations might, given time, have recovered even from the Bosnian crisis of 1908-9. As it was, the blow dealt to Russian confidence in Austrian intentions was so severe, and Russia's subsequent efforts to counter supposed Austrian designs by establishing her own control of the Balkan states so alarmed the Austrians, as to obscure even their common interest in monarchical solidarity. In the acrimonious diplomacy surrounding the redistribution of the Ottoman heritage in 1912-13 Austro-Russian relations plunged to new depths. As a result, the two Powers were quite unable to re-establish the relations of confidence that might have enabled them to cope with the crisis in July 1914.

It is true that the breakdown of Austro-Russian co-operation on several occasions in the past had not resulted in war. The two Powers had simply fallen back on diplomacy to promote their influence in the Balkan states and Turkey; the result had generally been a kind of balance in which each had managed to establish its predominance in one Balkan state or another, with Turkey serving both as a neutral buffer between the two rivals and a lightning-conductor for the territorial ambitions of the Balkan states. With the disappearance of Turkey-in-Europe, however, the Austrians found themselves suddenly confronted with an entirely new situation. It was not simply that the Balkan states were now stronger in terms of manpower and territory — Serbia, in particular, had more than doubled in size. Success had strengthened their confidence immensely and whetted their appetites; and now that Turkey was gone, their expansionist ambitions would have to take a new direction. Moreover, if they could ever combine together they would constitute, to all intents and purposes, a new Great Power — with a military potential of over a million men — that would give Austria-Hungary food for thought, especially if they could count on assistance from Russia.

This, too, seemed to be a serious possibility. Unlike the inert Ottoman Empire, concerned only to survive, the expansionist Balkan states were by no means disinclined to throw in their lot with a particular Great Power to further their ambitions. Indeed, in the nine months between the end of the Balkan wars and the Sarajevo assassinations, a whole series of French and Russian diplomatic successes in the Balkan capitals seemed to portend the creation of a new Balkan League under Russian auspices. The French were making good use of their influence as the bankers of Europe in Greece. In Bulgaria, France and Russia were striving insistently, if ultimately in vain, to make the granting of a new loan conditional on King Ferdinand's dismissing the Austrophile government, installed in the wake of Bulgaria's defeat at the hands of Serbia and her allies in the Second Balkan War. In June 1914, a spectacular visit by the Russian imperial family to Constantza cast doubt on the future of the Austro-Rumanian dynastic alliance and gave new heart to irredentist circles in Rumania whose eyes were fixed on Hungarian Transylvania. Serbia's ambitions were notorious: had not the Serbian premier, Pasic, himself declared during the Bucharest peace conference at the end of the Balkan wars, that having won 'the first round against Turkey', Serbia must prepare for the second against Austria-Hungary? Within months he was in St Petersburg where the Tsar assured him that Russia had not forgotten Serbia's brothers groaning under the Austro-Hungarian yoke. It was not surprising, therefore, that by the spring of 1914 the Austrians were becoming alarmed at rumours of a new Balkan combination — whereby Serbia and Rumania would make territorial concessions in the south to buy the support of Bulgaria and Greece, compensating themselves from the territories of the Monarchy. 'A revived Balkan League', the leading Viennese newspaper declared in February 1914, 'would be a dagger pointed at the heart of Austria.'

In the past, when Austro-Russian

relations had broken down and the Monarchy felt threatened, it had generally been able to turn for support to other Great Powers. This had usually enabled it to establish some kind of balance and to safeguard its interests by diplomatic means. British governments in the later nineteenth century, for example, had felt that Russian control of the Ottoman Empire might threaten Great Britain's communications with India. So the British had joined with the Austrians in 1878 to restrain Russia at the Congress of Berlin; for a decade after 1887 Italy worked with those two Powers in the Mediterranean Entente to resist the spread of Russian influence in the Ottoman Empire and the Balkans. In 1907, however, Great Britain and Russia had managed to agree about spheres of influence in Asia. Since then the British had been particularly anxious not to offend St Petersburg: British imperial interests ruled out any notion of bolstering the Austrian position in the Near East. There could be no return to the Mediterranean Entente.

By taking this attitude, it has been argued,[2] the British must bear some of the responsibility for the subsequent collapse of the balance and the catastrophe of 1914. If so, then Austria-Hungary's German ally must perhaps be given an even greater share. Throughout the 'seventies and 'eighties Bismarck had striven to cultivate Russia by supporting her in the Balkans. He had expressly warned the Austrians that the alliance of 1879 was not designed to support any Balkan policy whatever. Even under his successors it was only on rare occasions that the Dual Alliance proved of any assistance to Austria-Hungary in maintaining her position by

diplomacy. These interludes — in the early 1890s and during the Bosnian crisis — had been brief, and had been followed by German efforts to repair the wire to St Petersburg by ostentatiously withholding support from Austria-Hungary. The Germans had declared their return to this policy when the Kaiser met the Tsar at Potsdam in November 1910. During the Balkan wars Germany, for the sake of improving its relations with Great Britain, put quite brutal pressure on the Austrians to keep the peace and to acquiesce in what seemed to Vienna a dangerous strengthening of Serbia. Finally in 1913-14 the Kaiser, exaggerating the value of his dynastic connections with Bucharest and Athens, was actually striving to bring about a combination of the victors of the Balkan wars — Rumania, Greece and Serbia. This was playing directly into the hands of French and Russian diplomacy and only intensified the deepening feelings of impotence and despair in Vienna.

It is important to emphasise, however, that even in the summer of 1914, when all the resources on which they had relied to maintain their position in the past seemed to have failed them, the Austrians did not plan to save the situation by war. In June 1914 Berchtold was still planning to redress the balance by diplomatic means, namely by a determined effort to enlist German support for a co-ordinated diplomatic campaign to establish the influence of the Central Powers in at least some parts of the Balkans — Rumania, Bulgaria, and Turkey — and hold Serbia in check. This programme was set out in a long memorandum for the information of Berlin — the so-called Matscheko memorandum.[3] It goes far to refute the

- Vienna
- Budapest

AUSTRIA-HUNGARY

R. Save

R. Danube

Transylvania

ROUMANIA

R. Dniester

R. Prut

RUSSIA

- Belgrade
- Bucharest

Bosnia

SERBIA

BULGARIA

MONTENEGRO

- Sofia

BLACK SEA

ADRIATIC SEA

- Scutari
- Durazzo

ALBANIA

- Adrianople
- Constantinople

- Salonica

GREECE

AEGEAN SEA

OTTOMAN EMPIRE

- Athens

∞∞∞∞∞∞ Frontiers in 1913
●●●●●● Frontiers in 1912

0   *Miles*   150

0   *km*   150

Crete

THE BALKANS IN 1914

12

THE GROWTH OF RUSSIAN INFLUENCE IN THE BALKANS 1888-1914

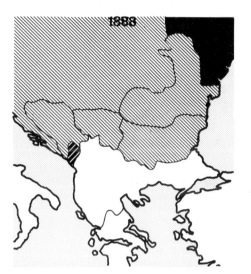

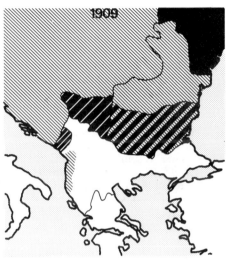

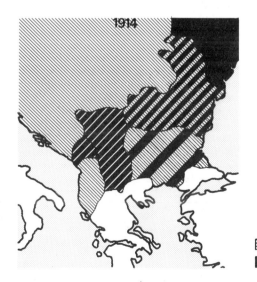

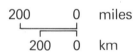

200   0   miles

200   0   km

Austro-Hungarian influence

Russian influence

charge that Austria-Hungary in the summer of 1914 was looking for pretexts to re-establish her position by war. The memorandum lay on Berchtold's writing table awaiting his signature when Archduke Franz Ferdinand set out for Sarajevo.

The Sarajevo assassinations radically transformed the situation. Serbian irredentism now appeared as a direct and immediate threat to the Habsburgs as lords of Bosnia, indeed, to the very existence of Austria-Hungary as a Great Power. To fail to act now, it seemed to Vienna, would be to give notice to the world that the Monarchy lacked even the will to survive; its enemies would be immeasurably heartened and the dreaded Balkan League would soon be on the scene. In these circumstances a laborious campaign of secret diplomacy, as outlined in the Matscheko memorandum, would no longer suffice. Strong action against Serbia was essential, as Berchtold put it, 'in the interests of our Great Power position'. Serbia must be presented with demands that would reduce her to the satellite status she had occupied in the days of the Austro-Serbian alliance of 1881-95; and if she refused to accept this voluntarily, force would be applied. In a sense, this was a defensive move: it was imperative, Berchtold told Berlin, 'for the Monarchy...to tear apart with a firm hand the threads which its opponents are seeking to form into a net above its head'. The condign punishment of Serbia — especially if Russia could be persuaded to accept it — would end the danger of a Balkan League under Russian auspices.

Here, however, the clash of the two defensive strategies came into play. Austria-Hungary's defensive bid for security had, from Russia's point of view, extremely offensive implications. The subjugation of Serbia would not merely put an end to the threat to the Monarchy; it would so overawe the other Balkan states as to deprive Russia, as Berchtold himself admitted, of 'all influence in the Balkans'. 'Russia can never swallow (*sich gefallen lassen*) this note under any circumstances,' Franz Joseph observed.[4] Here, clearly recognised, lay the danger of a war between the two Great Powers. Undeterred, Berchtold took the fateful step of revising the Matscheko memorandum, to turn it from a project for a long-term diplomatic campaign into a demand for immediate action against Serbia, and sent it off to Berlin on 5 July.

Certainly, the Austrians could not contemplate risking a war with Russia without an assurance of German support. Yet Germany's recent behaviour made it seem by no means certain that Germany would support her ally in a forward policy. In the spring of 1914, when the Austrians had talked of using force to prevent Serbia establishing herself on the Adriatic by absorbing Montenegro, the Kaiser had described them as 'crazy'. More recently the Germans had remained exasperatingly deaf to Austrian attempts to convince them of the reality of the threat from Serbia; and had urged Vienna instead to concentrate on conciliating Serbia by economic concessions. Hence the need for an Austrian enquiry in Berlin in July 1914. The German reply would be crucial.

Germany and the decision for war

The German reaction was to be a further step along the road towards an

Austro-Russian conflict. Germany herself was later to take the final step, with her declarations of war on Russia and France, in transforming the conflict into a continental war and provoking the intervention of Britain that started the World War. The motives behind the German decision of 5 July to present the Austrians with the fatal 'blank cheque' must now be considered.

The German decision, it must be emphasised, was in no sense determined by the terms of the dual alliance of 1879 — a purely defensive military agreement which contained no obligations whatever to give diplomatic support. In a more general sense, however, its very existence, and above all the fear of losing it, was of crucial importance. In the final crisis the solidarity of the Central Powers was more the product of their mutual mistrust than of *deutsche Treue*. Berchtold feared that if Austria-Hungary could not summon up the will to act against Serbia now, Germany might despair of her chances of survival and abandon the alliance. The Germans, for their part, were afraid that if, after all the friction and misunderstandings of the past three years they were to thwart their Austrian allies yet again, Austria-Hungary might finally lose patience with Germany and seek salvation in an entente with Russia; or she might lapse into complete apathy, virtually ceasing to exist as a Great Power. In either case the result would be the total isolation of Germany.

The answer to the question why Germany should on this occasion be so nervous about estranging Austria-Hungary — as compared with, say, in the 1880s or even as recently as 1912-

13 — cannot be given solely in terms of the Serbian crisis. It is true that the assassination of his good friend Franz Ferdinand had deeply upset William II himself, and had opened the eyes of Berlin to the reality of the Serbian threat to Austria-Hungary: 'the Serbs must be sorted out, and that very soon', the Kaiser declared. The critical factor was, however, that in the summer of 1914 German fears of isolation were infinitely more acute than at any time since the 1870s; and this was a result, not merely of the threat to Austria-Hungary, but of the recent development of Germany's relations with the other Powers.

From the German point of view the most ominous development on the international scene after 1912 was the growing power of Russia. The expulsion of Turkey from Europe by Russia's clients in the Balkan League was seen in Berlin as directly undermining Germany's military security. In the first place, in any future war the Austrians would now have to pay more attention to the threat from the south and would have correspondingly less to spare for joint operations with Germany in Poland. In the second, the Ottoman army, trained by German military missions since the 1880s and bidding fair by 1911 to draw off significant Russian forces from Poland to fight in the Caucasus, had proved another shattering disappointment. At the same time Germany, somewhat disillusioned with Weltpolitik after her defeat in the Moroccan crisis of 1911, was becoming increasingly concerned to build up her position in Central Europe and the Near East — where the vast majority of her external economic interests were concentrated. Berlin was therefore coming to regard Russian attempts to control the Balkans not simply as a threat to Austria-Hungary, but to Germany herself. The turn of 1913-14 saw the first direct clash between Russia and Germany at Constantinople when St Petersburg objected to German plans to reform the Ottoman army through the Liman von Sanders mission. In 1914 the Germans were finding it increasingly difficult to counter the efforts of Russia and her French financial backers to establish their influence in the Balkans. Germany, whose capital resources were largely absorbed by her own industry, was hard pressed to compete with France — whose peasant investors preferred to put their money in high-interest loans abroad — in providing loans for Balkan governments, most of whom seemed by the summer to be drifting into the Franco-Russian orbit. Even Turkey seemed a lost cause: the Liman von Sanders mission was not a success; the visit by a Turkish delegation to the Tsar at Livadia in May gave Berlin food for thought; and the German chancellor Bethmann Hollweg began to doubt the wisdom of lending money 'to sharpen the Turkish sabre for France and Russia'. Altogether, if Germany was now being drawn into opposition to Russia in the Near East, it was as much on her own account as on behalf of her ally.

Perhaps even more alarming was the simultaneous and startling expansion of Russia's military capacity. The speed with which Russia had recovered from the effects of the disasters of 1905 took the Germans completely by surprise: 'Russia is now better prepared for war than ever before' became the insistent refrain of German military planners in 1913-14. The German response to this was to restrict

expenditure on the navy and to go all out for a huge increase in the size of the army — ordered by the Kaiser in December 1912 and inaugurated with the army budget of 1913. But this only led Russia to intensify her own efforts and encourage France to do the same. The increasingly hectic tempo of the armaments race was echoed in strident press campaigns in Russia and Germany in the spring of 1914, which in turn only heightened the feeling in Berlin that war with Russia was now inevitable in the near future. 'If anybody doubts,' William II commented on one Russian newspaper article in June 1914, that Russia and France 'are preparing to attack Germany, he belongs in the lunatic asylum.' In this atmosphere there could be no question of Germany's attempting to humour Russia in Bismarckian fashion. 'Russo-Prussian relations are dead for ever,' William II declared in February. When, at this juncture, Sarajevo raised the question of the whole future of Austria-Hungary and the Near East, it seemed imperative, out of simple self-interest, that Germany should support her ally.

Germany's relations with the western Powers pointed to the same conclusion. France, for example, was not merely deeply involved in financing Russia's recent successes in the Balkans; she was irremediably hostile since the loss of Alsace-Lorraine in 1871, and herself posed a military threat to Germany. German military planners had assumed ever since 1872 that Germany would have to fight France and Russia together if ever she became involved in war with either; and from the time of Schlieffen (chief of staff, 1891-1905) it had been generally agreed that the best chance for Germany lay in first knocking out

France as the weaker partner — in six weeks if possible. Now the increase in the size of the French army portended by the introduction of three-year military service in 1913 — which would have brought the French army up to the strength of the German — posed as serious a threat as Russia's recent activities to the successful implementation of the Schlieffen plan. At least, as the Germans saw it, there was nothing to be gained from France by a policy of conciliation or delay.

The British, who the German military assumed would be bound to fight to keep the Belgian coast out of German control, were not regarded, in military terms, as a serious threat. The Kaiser and his civilian advisers, more in awe of British seapower, had nevertheless been making an effort since December 1912 to draw Great Britain away from her entente partners and secure her neutrality. (It was for this reason that they had been concerned to restrain Austria-Hungary from resorting to arms during the Balkan wars.) By the spring of 1914, however, the Germans were disappointed with the results of their diplomatic efforts: in the struggle for influence in the Near East, the British still refused to abandon France and Russia. True, Anglo-German relations were in themselves better than for several years: the naval race had lost much of its momentum with the German decision to concentrate on the army; and as the Anglo-German negotiations on the future of the Portuguese colonies showed in June 1914, imperialist rivalry had ceased to be an issue between London and Berlin. Indeed, to many people in Great Britain, the war seemed to come like lightning out of a clear sky. The Germans, however, were more impressed by the news that the British and Russians were in process of co-ordinating their naval strategies in the Baltic. They decided that the Triple Entente Powers were, after all, likely to move closer together in future.[5] Altogether, therefore, the cultivation of Great Britain, like the maintenance of the wire to St Petersburg, had ceased to provide the Germans with a motive for leaving Austria-Hungary in the lurch.

On 5 July the Kaiser, and on 6 July Bethmann Hollweg, endorsed Berchtold's plans and promised Germany's full support in the event of Russian intervention. The implications of this decision — given virtually over luncheon — were perhaps less clearly thought out than some historians have maintained. It is true that there were people in high places in Berlin who insisted that France and Russia were growing stronger day by day, and that they would certainly attack the central Powers when they were ready — probably by 1917; and some of these people actually advocated a preventive war. It was also undeniable that the German army, the active units of which had just completed their reorganisation under the 1913 programme, was in a relatively strong position that would not last for ever; that Austria-Hungary was growing weaker; that the whole position of the Central Powers in the Near East was steadily deteriorating while their chances of saving it by diplomacy were, to say the least, problematical. Moreover, in a crisis over the Near East, Austria-Hungary could be counted on to appear in the field — which had certainly not been the case in the Moroccan crisis of 1911. These ideas were all familiar to the German foreign minister, Jagow, when he stated the German position:

'we do not seek a preventive war, but if the challenge (*Kampf*) presents itself, we must not shrink from it'. Certainly, the Germans were prepared to contemplate war rather than tolerate a further deterioration of their position. Moreover, like the Austrian decision to risk a war with Serbia, the German decision to risk a European war was bound to have offensive implications from the point of view of the other Powers. A successful war would not merely put an end to a series of German diplomatic defeats; it would raise Germany to a dominant position in Europe once and for all.

Even so, in this plethora of calculations, offensive and defensive, the fact remains that the German assurances to Austria-Hungary on 5 July did not amount to a decision for war. It is important to note that the Germans coupled these assurances with the advice to Vienna to act quickly against Serbia, expressly on the grounds that the shock administered to the Tsar's feelings of monarchical solidarity by the assassination offered the best chance of restraining Russia from supporting the 'regicides'.[6] In other words, the Germans were still counting on the possibility of a diplomatic victory. If this could be achieved it would not only, as the Austrians calculated, tear apart the 'net' that was being spun in the Near East, it might well lead to a diplomatic revolution in Europe.[7] The pro-German extreme right-wing elements at the Russian court might at last prevail on the Tsar to abandon a policy of co-operation with the western Powers that brought Russia nothing but defeats and humiliation, and to return to a Three Emperors' Alliance. Now a restoration of the Three Emperors' Alliance would — as Great Britain and France indeed feared — give Germany the mastery of the continent without the risks of war. Certainly the Germans were prepared in the last resort to face those risks in July 1914; but a diplomatic victory which destroyed the opposing Power bloc would serve their purposes equally well.

As it turned out, the Germans had miscalculated. The Austrians did not act quickly against Serbia — their army could not be organised for serious military operations until mid-August anyway. Instead, they spent three weeks compiling a formidable dossier listing Serbia's violations of her promise to Europe to live as a good neighbour of Austria-Hungary — promises by which she had escaped an Austrian invasion in 1909. This dossier was presented in Belgrade on 23 July — as if legalistic arguments could carry any weight when vital interests of the Great Powers were at stake. On 25 July the Serbs replied, promising again to mend their ways and accepting most of the Austro-Hungarian demands; but they rejected the crucial stipulation that Austro-Hungarian officials be allowed to participate in controlling irredentist activity in Serbia itself. After all, this demand would have reduced Serbia from a sovereign state to a dependency of the Monarchy — as indeed it was intended to do. The Austrians, determined not to be fobbed off yet again with worthless promises, and above all determined to forestall any mediatory action by the Powers, such as had saved Serbia in the past, declared war on 28 July and bombarded Belgrade. It is worth noting that, in Berlin, William II had regarded the Serbian reply as a 'splendid victory. With this every reason for war disappears'. Even when the Austrians went ahead and declared war, he still suggested that they might stop after an initial military success and settle for a diplomatic victory — the famous 'halt in Belgrade' proposal of 29 July. However, all chance of a diplomatic victory for the Central Powers was about to disappear.

From the start, the Russians were aware of the implications of Austria-Hungary's actions against Serbia for their influence in the Near East, indeed, for their whole Great Power position. For this reason, they had refused to press Serbia to accept the Austrian terms. Once Austria-Hungary declared war on Serbia, the Russians made a more positive effort to save their reputation as protectors of the Balkan states. They demanded that the Austrians cease their military operations against Serbia and discuss possible modifications of the note of 24 July. It was in an effort to strengthen Russia's negotiating position that on 29 July the Tsar ordered a partial mobilisation — against Austria-Hungary. When it transpired that for technical reasons a partial mobilisation would make it more difficult to implement a full mobilisation should Germany after all intervene, the Tsar issued the order for full mobilisation on 30 July. It must be emphasised, however, that Nicholas II was perfectly sincere when he assured the Germans that not a single Russian soldier would cross the frontier unless Russia was herself attacked. Mobilisation was for the Russians a diplomatic move to demonstrate their determination not to abandon Serbia in the forthcoming negotiations with Austria-Hungary — which at this time were getting off to a faltering start. In Berlin, however, the news of Russian mobilisation had a devastating effect. Not only were the political implications clear — Russia

was not prepared to hand the Germans their diplomatic victory; the military implications suddenly confronted the Central Powers with the prospect of a shattering diplomatic defeat.

Already the news that Russia would not readily abandon Serbia had led by 28 July to a shift of opinion in Berlin towards contemplating the prospect of a continental war. This was the background to Bethmann Hollweg's gestures designed to secure British neutrality. On 30 July he advised Vienna not to reject out of hand a proposal of Grey's whereby Austria-Hungary should cease her military operations and put the Austro-Serbian dispute in the hands of the Concert. Yet this advice was immediately countermanded by Moltke, and Bethmann himself had been less concerned to prevent war than, as he explained to Berchtold, 'to push on to Russia the blame for the war that is now breaking out'.[8] Not that Berchtold would have been willing to invoke the Concert anyway. Indeed, he regarded its failures in 1913 as responsible for the whole deplorable situation in the Near East. But it was not the deadlock over the future of Serbia — still the subject of continuing if unfruitful discussions between Vienna and St Petersburg on 31 July — but the news of Russian mobilisation that precipitated the German decision to start a continental war.

The war plans of the German general staff in the summer of 1914 rested on the assumption that Germany's only hope of surviving — let alone winning — a war on two fronts was by a quick knock-out blow against France before Russia could bring the weight of her vast but cumbersome military machine to bear. The corollary of this was that if ever the Tsar's army stood fully mobilised on the German frontier — whether it actually launched an attack or not — Germany would no longer have any means of dealing with a Franco-Russian combination: she would be unable to go to war at all. This fact would itself predetermine the outcome of any negotiations the Central Powers might enter into over the Eastern question, whether direct or through the Concert. If Russia were allowed to complete her mobilisation, therefore, the Central Powers would not only be robbed of the diplomatic victory that would reverse the trend of events in the Near East; they would also suffer a more devastating diplomatic defeat than anything they had experienced in the past two years; one that would jeopardise their whole position as Great Powers. Hence the speed and decisiveness of the German reaction on 31 July — the peremptory demands to Russia to cease her mobilisation measures forthwith, and to France to give guarantees of good behaviour. Not surprisingly these demands — incompatible with the existence of Russia and France as Great Powers — were simply ignored in St Petersburg and Paris. Germany thereupon declared war on Russia and France and, in accordance with her military plans, marched into Luxemburg and Belgium.

The British, in the early stages of the crisis, had been concerned to keep in the background. If Austria-Hungary 'could make war on Serbia and at the same time satisfy Russia,' Grey told the Austro-Hungarian ambassador on 27 July, 'well and good: I could take a holiday tomorrow. But if not, the consequences would be incalculable.'9 Lacking any mandate from the Cabinet to commit Great Britain, he could only mark time and offer his good offices.

With the outbreak of the continental war, however, Great Britain faced a choice between neutrality and intervention on the side of France and Russia. The military and naval talks held with the French since 1905 had been designed to make British intervention possible; but Grey had always been careful to emphasise that they in no sense constituted a commitment to intervene; and Great Britain had no obligations to assist Russia at all. Yet just as Germany had felt compelled in her own interests to support Austria-Hungary beyond the stipulations of the dual alliance, so the British were concerned at all costs to hold on to the understandings they had reached with France and Russia. 'If we fail [Russia]...now,' the ambassador in St Petersburg had warned on 24 July, 'we cannot hope to maintain that friendly co-operation with her in Asia that is of such vital importance to us.' Moreover, it was essential to maintain the independence of France and Russia as elements in the European balance of power. If Germany gained control of the continent she might proceed to threaten the British empire. In brief, Grey had no desire to see a neutral Great Britain standing alone after the war was over, against an expansionist Germany or an embittered France and Russia. As he told parliament on 3 August, 'if we are engaged in war, we shall suffer but little more than we shall suffer even if we stand aside'. There was a slight delay before the Liberal Cabinet could be brought round but on 4 August the British government, citing its rights as a guarantor of Belgian neutrality under the treaty of 1839, demanded that Germany withdraw her troops from Belgium. When this was refused Britain declared war on Germany. The continental war had become a world war.†

The debate over the causes of the war

The consequences of the First World War were so cataclysmic that it is hardly surprising that its origins have been intensely debated ever since. The victorious allies, in an attempt to justify the penalties imposed on the defeated, put the blame fairly and squarely in the famous war-guilt article of the Treaty of Versailles, on 'the aggression of Germany and her allies'. Not unnaturally, the Germans, in their campaign to revise the Treaty in the inter-war years, led the attack on this theory. They drew heart from revisionist statements from Entente circles, such as Lloyd George's confession that 'we all slithered into it'. With the publication of the great collections of documents from the pre-war foreign offices, historians came forward to put the blame on almost every Power in turn. Others attributed the catastrophe to more general causes: the rigid system of alliances — or its opposite — 'international anarchy'; the conflicts of economic imperialism; and the accumulation of armaments. More recently it has been argued — especially in Germany — that growing domestic difficulties were pushing some governments to try to solve their problems by an external war. Yet it must be admitted that all of these factors had been operating in the forty years of peace before 1914. Although all of them have some bearing on the question, none of them will in itself explain why the international system broke down in that fatal summer.

Alliances and ententes

As far as the network of alliances is concerned, it must immediately be said that no government in July and August 1914 acted in fulfilment of its treaty obligations; and the British did not even have any. Indeed, far from being a cause of war, the alliances and ententes that had developed in Europe since 1879 had helped to give the continent half a century of peace — that is, so long as they operated to give the Powers concerned the sense of security that is essential to the diplomacy of compromise, or served as deterrents to reckless actions. The causes of the war must be sought, rather, in the decay of the alliance system in the years of crisis after 1912 — in Germany's loss of faith in the strength of her alliances and growing obsession with the threat of isolation; in Great Britain's fears for the fragility of the Ententes. After all, the alliances and ententes were merely the formal symbols of great common interests. It was the determination to protect these interests at all costs that so restricted the options of Germany and Great Britain in 1914 and led them to give their partners support far in excess of any treaty obligations. To blame 'secret diplomacy' or 'the system of alliances' for the war is to mistake the symptom for the disease.

Imperialism

Nor can 'imperialist rivalry' as a general term — any more than 'national pride' or 'original sin' — explain why a states system that had functioned peacefully for over a generation suddenly broke down in 1914. For the most part, in fact, the extra-European activities of the Great Powers in the era of imperialist expansion after 1880 had little to do with the outbreak of war. After all, the Powers who had been the chief rivals in that period fought on the same side in 1914 — against a Germany that seemed largely to have abandoned any interest in *Weltpolitik*. True, once the war started, the exponents of Weltpolitik were once again allowed a voice in defining the aims of Germany policy. Indeed, in all the belligerent countries an eventual victory was seen as an opportunity to acquire, among other things, enemy colonies. But this was a consequence, not a cause of the outbreak of war.

In one particular area, however, imperialist rivalry was an important contributory factor to the outbreak of war: the Near East. There, it was one element in the collapse of the position of the Central Powers that lay at the root of the threatening revolution in the balance of power that led to the resort to arms. Indeed, Germany's very withdrawal from the struggle overseas after the disappointments of the Second Moroccan Crisis was accompanied by her increasing concentration on areas where she still had great economic interests at stake and some hope of success: Austria-Hungary, the Balkans, and Asia Minor. Here, the importance of Italy's imperialist war against the Ottoman Empire in Libya (1911-12) can hardly be exaggerated. Insofar as it helped to precipitate the Balkan Wars and the expulsion of Turkey from Europe, it undermined the stability of the entire Near East. Even in Austria-Hungary's case, the obstinate refusal of her German and Italian allies in 1913-14 to accommodate her imperialist aspirations on the south coast of Asia Minor at the expense of their own spheres of influence there intensified the frustration that had been building up in Vienna since the end of the Balkan Wars.[10] After 1913 the steady growth of Russian influence throughout the whole area, ably assisted by French financial imperialism, brought home to the Germans the seriousness of the threat to their economic interests there. It was partly for the sake of these interests that Germany was fighting in 1914.

As for the Triple Entente Powers, it might be argued that it was the success of France and Russia in peacefully penetrating the Near East that provoked Vienna and Berlin to seek to redress the balance by war. On the other hand, the very fact that those two Powers were doing so well by diplomacy meant that they were not in the least inclined to think in terms of war to further their economic objectives. Moreover, even after 1907 Russia was continuing her imperialistic expansion in Asia, and above all in Persia; but although this caused some irritation in London, it never threatened to lead to war. Certainly, the concessions Russia had had to make to Japan in the Far East, and to Great Britain in Central Asia and Persia in the wake of the Russo-Japanese war did nothing to diminish her sensitivity about seeing herself hemmed in by the Central Powers in the Near East. But her concern for the Balkans was not motivated by economic imperialism — that was merely the means to the end — but by anxiety for the security of the Straits. In the case of Great Britain, past conflicts over imperialist issues were only indirectly a cause of the war. Incidents such as the Kaiser's telegram to Kruger, and, more important, Germany's clashes with France over Morocco, had perhaps helped to establish in the Foreign Office the frame of mind that instinctively regarded Germany as a threat to the British empire and to the independence of France, and thereby to influence British decisions in 1914. More important in determining British entry into the war, however, was the sense of immense relief that the threats from Great Britain's old imperial rivals had been banished in 1904 and 1907, and the concomitant fear that if Great Britain left France and Russia in the lurch, the old struggles would resume. The British were perhaps not so much engaged in an imperialist conflict in 1914 as seeking to avoid one.

Armaments

The view that the accumulation of armaments in Europe had in itself caused the war was one that found widespread currency in the inter-war years when it was used to some effect, in Great Britain at least, by the opponents of rearmament. Yet the general assertion that arms races in themselves cause wars cannot be sustained: the Anglo-French naval race of the 1880s, for example, did not result in war; and conversely, it might be argued that if there had been an arms race in the 1930s it might have helped to prevent a war. Even in the case of 1914 the importance of one particular arms race — the naval race between Great Britain and Germany — should not be exaggerated. Indeed, it seems that the unpleasant prospect of fighting a superior British fleet was a factor in deciding the Germans to refrain from attacking France in the Moroccan crisis of 1911.[11] True, the destruction of the German fleet, like the acquisition of German colonies, became an objective of British policy once the war had started. But the most that can be said of naval rivalry before the war is that — like the friction over Morocco — it contributed to establishing the image of Germany as an enemy that persisted in London

long after naval rivalry, the chief bone of contention between Great Britain and Germany between 1908 and 1912, had itself ceased to be an issue. It had also perhaps contributed to the division of Europe into two armed camps. The British did not view the German fleet in isolation:[12] after 1909 even Italy and Austria-Hungary were building Dreadnoughts; and the prospect that the German fleet might find even greater reinforcements elsewhere only intensified British determination to uphold France and Russia as independent Great Powers. On the German side, the news of impending Anglo-Russian naval talks in the summer of 1914 perhaps made Berlin rather more nervous at the prospect of encirclement; but by that time the Germans were above all preoccupied with the armaments that France and Russia were building up on land.

As regards the military establishments of the continental Great Powers, the critics of the 'merchants of death' can make a stronger case. For the continental Powers, unlike Great Britain, the war can be seen not as a bolt from the blue, but as the deluge from a storm cloud that had been building up with frightening intensity since about 1912. Here again, it must be conceded that ever since the German war-machine had demonstrated its proficiency in 1870, the continental Powers had been striving to maintain great armaments in peacetime; and that this had not led to war. On the contrary, the military superiority of the — essentially conservative — Triple Alliance Powers in the 1880s had been a factor making for peace; just as the fact that German military planners considered the army unprepared for war had deterred the more reckless elements in Berlin from launching a preventive war against France in 1905.[13] Similarly, Russia's military inferiority to the Central Powers after the Russo-Japanese war had obliged her to accept a diplomatic defeat in the Bosnian crisis of 1909. After about 1912, however, the balance of military power ceased to operate as a restraining factor in the states system.

In the first place, the armaments sold over the years to the Balkan states by the Great Powers — and here Germany was as heavily involved as her opponents — were at last put to use, with devastating effects on the balance of power in south-east Europe. The consequences of these changes, taken together with the new armaments programmes of France, and, above all, Russia, in turn caused profound alarm in Berlin. In December 1912 the Germans determined on a desperate effort to strengthen their own army in preparation for an armed confrontation that was now felt — in military and civilian circles alike — to be inevitable in the very near future. It is true that for a year or so, so long as the German army was in the throes of reorganisation, this served as an additional incentive to Berlin to restrain the Austrians from resorting to arms in the Balkan upheavals of 1913. By March 1914, however, the German chief of staff, von Moltke, was declaring that, from a purely military point of view, Germany's chances were now good, and that the sooner war came, the better.

Even so, such language had been heard in Berlin on earlier occasions — in 1888, 1905 and 1912 — and war had not broken out. The feeling that war was a perfectly natural activity for independent states, and indeed, in times of crisis, the feeling that war was imminent, were characteristic of the 'unspoken assumptions' that underlay the behaviour of Europeans ever since the rise of sovereign states.[14] The view that national honour and 'vital interests' must in the last resort be defended on the battlefield was by no means confined to the great military monarchies of eastern Europe. Perhaps it was always more marked in Prussia, a state that owed its greatness entirely to military success; but it was reinforced, throughout Europe, at the end of the nineteenth century by crude notions of social Darwinism and talk of an impending struggle of the nations for supremacy over the world. On the whole, such feelings ebbed and flowed according to the degree of tension on the international scene. They certainly reached a peculiar intensity in Germany, and were reflected in the unprecedented increases in the armaments programmes of all the continental Powers in the years of crisis after 1912. They affected not merely the Kaiser and his military advisers but even the pacific Bethmann Hollweg, who now discerned a 'doom' (*Fatum*) hanging over Europe; and who decided not to plant any more trees on his East Prussian estates, because the Russians would be there in fifty years' time.[15]

All this is not to say, however, that in 1914 the German government was set on war and looking for a pretext. As has been seen, the decision for war was only taken when Russian mobilisation presented Berlin with a choice between war and diplomatic defeat. But the frantic arms race of 1912-14 was undoubtedly a factor in the crisis, insofar as by the summer of 1914 the armies of Germany, France and Russia were all better prepared for war than ever before; and the governments of those states felt correspondingly less inclined to accept a major political defeat.

The decline of concert diplomacy

The view that the war was the result of 'international anarchy', although popular among supporters of the League of Nations in the inter-war years, encounters the same objection as the other general theories discussed above: that it must also account for the long peace after 1871. It might also be objected that the Great Powers of Europe in fact conducted their relations in a way far removed from anarchy — or at any rate in a less anarchical fashion than their twentieth-century successors. Before 1914 international relations were in the hands of a small group of men, all of whom shared the same culture, knew the rules of the game, appreciated the distinction between non-vital interests, which were negotiable, and vital interests, which were not, and had developed a highly sophisticated routine for reconciling their conflicting interests short of war. Sometimes this was done through the 'Concert of Europe' of all the Great Powers, sometimes through limited agreements between potential opponents. The success of the 'old diplomacy' in peacefully containing that potentially most dangerous clash of interests — in the Near East — for over half a century is in itself proof that the relations between the Great Powers rested on something other than 'international anarchy'.

In fact, an element of anarchy — in the sense of the absence of binding ties between states — could sometimes make for peace, or at least for the restriction of wars to the two or three Powers directly concerned in a dispute. This had been the case in the quarter century between the end of the Crimean War and the conclusion of the first of the great alliances in 1879. Equally, the clear preponderance of a group of conservative Powers, such as that of Great Britain and the Triple Alliance in the 1880s, could also make for peace; as could a flexible and complex balance of three groups with links between them, such as existed in the decade around the turn of the century. After about 1911, however, the European Powers gradually aligned themselves into two fairly evenly balanced blocs, with each striving to ensure its own security regardless of the effects of its actions on the security of the other. The problem facing the European states system was not anarchy but polarisation.

The growing tendency to resort to violence, as seen in the wars of 1911-13 against the Ottoman empire, itself generated feelings of nervousness and insecurity that were prejudicial to the functioning of the Concert of Europe. The consequence of these wars, the overthrow with appalling suddenness, of the Near Eastern balance of power with which statesmen had grown familiar over the past 50 years, induced an atmosphere of something approaching panic in the chancelleries of Europe. By January 1912 the long-experienced permanent under-secretary in the Foreign Office, Sir Arthur Nicolson, had 'never seen the world in such a disturbed condition'. Everywhere fear replaced trust, deepening the suspicion between the two groups of Powers. Gradually the links between them that had enabled the Concert to function in the past broke down: the London conference of 1912-13, at which Great Britain and Germany co-operated to impose a compromise settlement in the Balkans was the last triumph of the Concert. It was also a hollow one. Its very success in forcing Austria-Hungary to acquiesce, time and again, in the expansion of the Balkan states, had exhausted the patience of that Power — all the more so when the Concert proved unable to compel Serbia and Montenegro to respect its restrictions on their ambitions. In both cases, however, the clear threat of Austro-Hungarian military action brought those states to heel (in May and October 1913). From this the Austrians drew the dangerous conclusion that salvation lay not in appeals to the Concert but in independent action and threats of war. After Sarajevo the Germans came round to the same view. Already since the spring of 1914 the Triple Entente Powers had co-ordinated their diplomatic strategy in the Balkans without consulting the Triple Alliance Powers. By July the Concert of Europe had in fact ceased to function in the Near East and the two blocs of Powers stood face to face.

It is of course true that the alignments of the Powers had changed often enough in the past. Even in 1914 it was not impossible that, given time, friction over Russia's attempts to extend its control of Persia might drive London and St Petersburg apart again; that Germany might abandon Austria-Hungary as a lost cause and seek to re-establish a conservative alliance with Russia. Given time, even the dangerous tensions that had built up by the summer of 1914 might have been dissipated by another diplomatic revolution. Time, however, was what the Powers were not given. Within a

matter of mere months after the end of the Balkan wars, the almost fortuitous events at Sarajevo suddenly produced a situation in which one or the other of the blocs of Powers faced a colossal diplomatic defeat. To Vienna and Berlin it now seemed that inaction would mean the total collapse of Austria-Hungary's Great Power position — and of any hopes that had been entertained until then of saving it by diplomacy; a successful action by the Central Powers would equally inevitably entail the total destruction of Russia's diplomatic position — which St Petersburg could hardly accept without a fight. However the chancelleries might manoeuvre, there was no escaping this. In the circumstances of the time, the problem hardly admitted of a peaceful solution.

Domestic politics and the decisions for war

It is insofar as they contributed to those 'circumstances of the time' that the domestic problems of the Great Powers, like the other general factors discussed above, are of relevance to the causes of the war.

Austria-Hungary

In Austria-Hungary's case, for example, much has been made of the stubborn refusal of the Habsburgs to conciliate the south Slavs and grant them anything like equality in the constitutional structure of the Monarchy. After all, until 1912 at least, there were far more south Slavs inside the Monarchy than in Serbia; a wise policy might have drawn the weaker element into a position of dependency on the stronger and Serbia would have ceased to be a problem. If the chance existed — and it is debatable whether any amount of 'reform' can assuage such an irrational force as nationalism — it was certainly missed. Franz Joseph simply shrank from the conflict with the Magyars that any attempt to weaken Hungary's position in favour of the south Slavs would have involved. Certainly, the harsh Magyarisation policies of Hungary had helped to destroy the Austro-Serbian alliance of 1881-95; and to vitiate the Austro-Rumanian alliance. To that extent they contributed to the feelings of isolation and despair that prevailed in Vienna in July 1914. But in the last analysis, Austro-Hungarian desperation stemmed from what was seen as an external threat to the Great Power position of the Monarchy.

The internal condition of the Monarchy in 1914 hardly constituted a conclusive argument for action. In the early years of the century the great crisis between Franz Joseph and the Magyars, that had almost reached the proportions of a civil war, had certainly been a conclusive argument against indulging in adventures. In 1914 the obstreperousness of the Czechs (which had led to the suspension of both the Parliament in Vienna and the Diet in Prague by the summer) and the discontents of the south Slavs, were a far less serious matter. They could be contained by the coercive power normally available to the dynasty. This was, in a sense, an argument for keeping the peace: war would both preoccupy the Army abroad and encourage foreign Powers to meddle in the Monarchy's national problems. On the other hand, the feeling that, if the government showed weakness in the face of Serbia, the south Slavs would become more troublesome at home, was perhaps an incentive for action in 1914. Militarily

the Monarchy was relatively well prepared: in October 1912 the Hungarian parliament had consented, after resisting for more than twenty years, to a significant increase in the size of the Common Army. Moreover, the growing strength of Russia and the Balkan states suggested that the position would deteriorate as time went on. These were arguments for action in 1914. On the other hand, the emperor had for years been ignoring the impetuous demands of the chief of staff, Conrad von Hoetzendorff, for a pre-emptive war against one or other of the Monarchy's neighbours. In June 1914 the emperor and his advisers were still set on an attempt to secure the Monarchy's interests by diplomacy. In the July crisis, the Hungarian prime minister, Tisza, fearing that a defeat would destroy the Monarchy, whereas a victorious war might both burden the Monarchy with yet more Slav subjects, and dangerously strengthen centralist forces against Budapest, argued strongly against a military solution. In the end, however, a combination of pressure from Berlin and his own indignation at the continued ravings of the Serbian press, made him swallow his misgivings. In the last resort it was not the domestic situation but external factors that determined the decisions of the statesmen of the Monarchy.

Germany

As regards Germany, the case has been more forcefully argued, especially in the last twenty years or so,[16] for seeing the decision for war in 1914 in terms of tensions within the social structure of the empire. It is now fairly generally accepted that the creators of the German empire of 1871 largely succeeded in their aim of ensuring that political control remained in the hands of the conservative, military-aristocratic elite that had previously controlled Prussia. This elite recognised, however — as did its counterpart in even more reactionary Russia — that the empire must develop its industrial potential if it was to survive as a Great Power. The resultant rapid industrialisation indeed made Germany the strongest Power in Europe by 1900; but it also brought great problems for the traditional elite. The Liberal critics of the regime, who demanded a government responsible to the Reichstag, were soon overshadowed, as the industrial proletariat steadily grew in numbers, by the Social Democrats, a movement dedicated — in theory at least — to outright revolution, and by 1913 the largest party in the Reichstag. Rather than attempt to compromise with these elements the regime — so recent historians have argued — resorted to diversionary tactics in the field of foreign policy, both to outflank the Left and to rally the propertied classes who were unfortunately at loggerheads over the rival claims of agriculture and industry in the German economy.

In the 1880s, for example, even the anti-colonialist Bismarck embarked briefly on imperialist expansion when the Right had temporarily lost control of the Reichstag. (The high tariff on grain, introduced in 1879 to protect the incomes of Prussian landowners, had resulted in high bread prices, alienating both workers and industrialists.) From the later 'nineties Weltpolitik and naval expansion were taken up, not merely to reconcile the industrialists to the protection of agriculture, but to create a popular national movement that might even replace the Reichstag as the forum of German politics. By 1909, however, the failure of these tactics was clear.

With the introduction of the Dreadnought in 1906, the cost of naval expansion had become prohibitive. Indeed, the attempt to raise extra revenue to finance it had reopened and deepened the rift between the agrarian and industrialist supporters of the regime. By 1912 the German government decided to abandon Weltpolitik and the naval race and concentrate on more immediate issues: the threat to its interests in the Near East, and the need to build up its armaments in Europe. On the domestic front, absolute deadlock prevailed: the government shrank from a *coup d'état*, but it remained as determined as ever not to yield an inch to the demands of the majority parties in the Reichstag for constitutional reform. In this situation a war would offer the regime a golden opportunity to rally the nation behind it. Even the Social Democrats would support a war to defend civilisation against Tsarist hordes — just as they had readily voted for increased armaments in 1913; and the prospect of establishing Germany's supremacy in the world once and for all would silence the growing criticism from Pan-German elements on the Right, whose appetites the government had so incautiously aroused, but not satisfied, in the era of Weltpolitik.

Now it is true that the shifts to which the German government had resorted, ever since 1871, to reinforce its position at home had weakened its position abroad. The annexation of Alsace-Lorraine — essentially a move by Bismarck to glorify the monarchy and dish the nationalists — had made a permanent enemy of France. The challenge to Great Britain implied in the naval programme, and Germany's challenges to France in North Africa still had a lingering influence on British assessments of German intentions in 1914. The heavy tariffs and the restrictive financial measures by means of which Bismarck sought to protect Prussian landowners east of the Elbe from the competition of Russian grain exports had driven even the reactionary Alexander III to turn to the French Republic for the capital that was essential for Russia's military and industrial development. By 1914 France and Russia were bound together by strong financial ties. Conversely, an acrimonious debate over German attempts to force Russia to renew the disadvantageous commercial treaty imposed on her in the hour of her defeat in 1905, was again poisoning Russo-German relations.[17]

Yet it was not such issues, but the perceived external threat from the alarming developments in south east Europe coupled with the rapid development of French and Russian military potential that motivated the German armaments programme of 1913. As German nervousness about the threat grew, so did the German obsession with the need for speed and for the absolutely smooth running of the war machine. Thus, in January 1913, alternative mobilisation plans for a war against Russia alone were finally discarded, so that the military planners could concentrate all their efforts on perfecting the Schlieffen plan. Internal decisions of this kind did indeed restrict the government's options in an external crisis. Henceforth, if the point was reached where Russia mobilised, German military planning would take over from diplomacy and the great war would start in East and West. That is still not to say that the German government desired a war. In the

spring of 1914 the Kaiser had still been unwilling to support any Austrian adventures. Yet when, in July, the Kaiser and his advisers were faced with a choice between supporting Austria-Hungary and accepting a diplomatic defeat, there was nothing in the internal situation in Germany to make them shrink from the risks of war, perhaps even a good deal to push them on.

Russia

The domestic situation in Russia must be considered, insofar as it was the Emperor's decision to oppose the Central Powers, even to the point of ordering general mobilisation, that actually provoked the German declaration of war. Certainly there were elements in the decision-making apparatus in Russia — a few ministers, elder statesmen like Witte, extreme Right-wing circles at court — who feared that war would bring revolution They argued, therefore, that Russia should at all costs avoid provoking the Central Powers, indeed, that she would do well to align herself with them in the cause of monarchical solidarity. These people were not all-powerful even at court, however; several members of the imperial family had married into the Serbian, Montenegrin, or Greek, royal houses; and Nicholas II himself had spoken sharply to an Austrian ambassador who tried to remind him of his obligation to monarchical solidarity: 'Moi aussi, je suis Slave'. Moreover, the power of those conservative elements who had always been the mainstay of co-operation with the Central Powers had been undermined by the establishment of a constitutional regime in 1905. Since then, liberal and nationalist views had been freely voiced — on foreign affairs at least — in the Duma and the press; and they had undoubtedly exerted an influence on Russian foreign policy, pushing it in the direction of co-operation with the western Powers and support for Russia's Slav protégés in the Balkans.

At the same time, the constitution of 1905 had failed to satisfy educated opinion; and the problems of developing an advanced industrial economy within the framework of a military-aristocratic monarchy had led to even greater tensions in Russia than in Germany. The state visit of President Poincaré to Russia in July 1914 was marred by a wave of great strikes in the capital. The Russian government, therefore, like the German, was by 1914 casting round for support. It could not afford to alienate the moderates further by abandoning the Slav cause. In St Petersburg, as in Vienna, there were those who argued that a defeat over the Serbian question, if it did not lead to revolution, would seriously impair the government's prestige and make the domestic situation more difficult to handle. But here again, for the government, the threat was essentially an external one: if the Central Powers were allowed to destroy Serbia, they would control not only the Balkans but the Straits. Russia would be reduced from a Great Power to a mere dependency of Vienna and Berlin. This was what was at stake for the Tsarist government. The alternative to risking the consequences of general mobilisation was Russia's abdication as a Great Power.

France

Of all the continental governments, that in Paris was perhaps the least subject to internal pressures in favour of war. Although France was the only Great Power with a territorial claim against another and, although if war broke out, the implementation of that claim would immediately become a war aim, no one in France seriously proposed to start a war on that account — if only because neither Russia nor Great Britain would support it. The French prime minister in 1914, Viviani, was a man of sincere pacifist convictions; and on the Left, dominant in the assembly, the critics of the three-year military service law were vocal enough to raise hopes in Berlin that the new programme might have to be abandoned. There were, however, currents in the Third Republic pulling strongly in the opposite direction: the financiers and industrialists and the nationalist Right. It has been argued[18] that, like the ruling elite in Germany, these circles had developed a taste for diversionary tactics to preserve the status quo: the Dreyfus affair, for example, and the great campaign against the Church, served to distract the Left from pressing for social reform. After 1905, however, these were dead issues, and the 'Intérêts' that controlled the Third Republic had to cast around for another cause to divert attention from the demands of the Left. This was found in nationalism. Its success was seen in the Second Moroccan crisis, which greatly heightened the public's awareness of the German menace and swept the Lorrainer Poincaré to the premiership in January 1912 and to the Presidency of the Republic a year later. With the outbreak of actual war in 1914, of course, reform could be postponed for the duration.

In foreign policy the new wave of nationalism was reflected in a more assiduous cultivation of the Russian alliance, and in increased support for Russia's activities in the Near East. French firms such as Schneider-Creusot were prominent in the arming of the Balkan states; and by the end of 1912 the French were promising Russia their full support even if she felt obliged to take the offensive to stop an Austrian advance in the Balkans. Millions of French peasant investors had an interest in the survival of Russia, come what may. It has been argued that France might have made greater efforts to restrain Russia in the final crisis.[19] But the action of the French ambassador at St Petersburg, Paléologue, on 30 July in simply refusing to pass on to the Russians the cautionary advice of Viviani to delay mobilisation was perhaps itself only a reflection of the deep divisions in French political society. In the event, however, the action of France, too, was determined not by domestic strains and stresses but by the external threat. The German demand for a pledge of neutrality (to be followed by the handing over to Germany of the eastern fortresses as guarantees of good behaviour) might just conceivably have been the last chance to stave off the implementation of the Schlieffen plan and a German declaration of war. But it was even more clearly a demand for the abdication of France as a Great Power. To that, not even the pacific government of Viviani could submit.

Great Britain

In Great Britain, as has been seen, the issues were clear enough to the small circle that directed foreign policy — Grey, the Foreign Office, and a coterie of their supporters in the Cabinet. The difficulty was that Grey, secretive and shy of confrontation, had only rarely felt moved to defend or even explain his policy to the Liberals on the back benches or the general public. (He could always count on Unionist votes to carry his policy in parliament.) As a result, a considerable element of Liberal opinion remained either ill-informed about foreign affairs or positively hostile to a policy that was, as even the former Lord Chancellor Loreburn agreed, 'a mere revival of the old Palmerstonian doctrine of the balance of power...rotten to the core'. Moreover, in practice, the decision over war and peace rested not with Grey and the Foreign Office but with the Cabinet and, ultimately, with parliament. As late as 2 August the Cabinet was almost equally divided on the issue of intervention. It seemed for a moment that the internal situation in Great Britain might indeed have a determining effect on her policy.

Other domestic factors came to Grey's aid, however. The Liberal government, already dependent on Irish votes since the elections of 1910, was steadily losing popularity as social and industrial unrest increased and Ireland drifted towards civil war. When Grey threatened to resign if the Cabinet refused to sanction intervention, he was in effect threatening his colleagues with the prospect of a coalition government of Liberal imperialists and Unionists (interventionists to a man) that would take Britain into the war anyway; and with the subsequent annihilation of the Liberal party as an effective political force. Faced with this, the opposition in the Cabinet collapsed at once; and Grey was able to exploit the German violation of Belgian neutrality to add a finishing touch to the presentation of his case to the Commons. In Great Britain's case, the domestic issue had only been whether the country would go to war on 4 August under a Liberal government or a few days later under a Coalition. Nevertheless, the issue of intervention itself was still essentially decided, as in the case of the continental Powers, in terms of Great Britain's state interests as an independent Great Power.

Conclusion

In conclusion, therefore, it would seem that all the belligerents of 1914 were motivated primarily by a defensive concern to protect their status as Great Powers — a status which they felt to be exposed to unacceptable external threats. In Austria-Hungary's case the war indeed arose, as Bernadotte Schmitt observed in his Historical Association pamphlet over thirty years ago, from the incompatibility between national aspirations and dynastic frontiers. This had also been the case when Austria had embarked on the limited wars of 1859 and 1866. The crisis of 1914 was infinitely more serious simply because the implications of Austria-Hungary's actions affected the vital interests of all the Great Powers of Europe.

These general explanations will not, however, explain why the international system collapsed in 1914 and not before. After all, the conflict between nationalism and dynasticism in Eastern Europe had caused problems, but not a European War, for over a century; and if the mere existence of rivalry between sovereign states is an explanation for war, there would have been no peace in Europe since the sixteenth century. More particularly, for over 40 years after 1871, the states system of Europe had provided for the peaceful adjustment of precisely those conflicting interests that in 1914 caused the war. It was indeed the purpose of the system developed by the Powers for conducting their relations to contain their rivalry without recourse to war. For most of the time, the arrangements adopted by the Powers — the Concert, alliances, the balance of armaments, spheres of economic predominance, and perhaps, above all, the creation of an atmosphere in which no Power felt that another was set on its total destruction — all this served to preserve the peace and limit the effects of adjustments to the status quo.

After about 1912, however, the international system for the peaceful containment of potential conflicts began to break down. The cataclysmic overthrow, with such frightening suddenness, of the balance in the Near East — in its territorial, military, and economic aspects — put a strain on the international system that would have taken years to accommodate. The immediate repercussions were felt in an unparalleled heightening of tension and nervousness, an unprecedented acceleration of the armaments race, and a loss of confidence in the machinery by which the Powers had adjusted their differences by diplomacy in the past. In this charged atmosphere, the assassinations at Sarajevo precipitated a situation that posed threats to the vital interests of almost all the Great Powers. Although, during the ensuing war, all developed expansionist ambitions at the expense of their enemies, or even allies, each could argue with some plausibility that it had gone to war for essentially defensive reasons.

Chronological Table

1911
June-November: Second Moroccan Crisis (French Protectorate proclaimed, February 1912)
28 September: Italy declares war on Ottoman Empire (Treaty of Lausanne, ceding Libya to Italy, 18 October 1912)

1912
8-18 October: Outbreak of First Balkan War, of Montenegro, Bulgaria, Serbia, and Greece against the Ottoman empire (Treaty of London, 30 May 1913)
8 December: 'War council' at Potsdam
17 December: Start of ambassadors' meetings at London (until 11 August 1913)

1913
29 June: Outbreak of Second Balkan War, of Greece and Serbia, and later Turkey and Rumania, against Bulgaria (Treaty of Bucharest, 10 August)
30 June: Army and Finance Bills introduced in German Reichstag
July-August: French law increasing military service from two to three years
18 October: Austro-Hungarian ultimatum to Serbia
November-January 1914: Liman von Sanders crisis

1914
April: British state visit to Paris (leading to Anglo-Russian naval talks)
14 June: Russian state visit to Rumania
24 June: Matscheko Memorandum drafted in Vienna
28 June: Sarajevo assassinations
5 July: Austria-Hungary appeals to Germany for support
23 July: Austro-Hungarian ultimatum (48 hours) presented to Belgrade
25 July: Serbian reply to Austria-Hungary
27 July: Austria-Hungary breaks off diplomatic relations with Serbia
28 July: Austria-Hungary declares war on Serbia
29 July: Russia declares general, then partial, mobilisation
30 July: Austro-Russian conversations resumed; Russia declares general mobilisation
31 July: German ultimatum (12 hours) to Russia; enquiry at Paris as to French attitude
1 August: French reply to Germany and (3.55 p.m.) mobilisation
4.00 p.m. German mobilisation
7.00 p.m. Germany declares war on Russia
2 August: Germany invades Luxemburg and demands permission (refused) to enter Belgium
3 August: Germany declares war on France, and starts invasion of Belgium
4 August: Germany declares war on Belgium; Great Britain declares war on Germany
6 August: Austria-Hungary declares war on Russia
12 August: Great Britain and France declare war on Austria-Hungary

Notes

† Only on 6 August did German pressure bring Austria-Hungary — more interested in consolidating her position in the Balkans that in relieving her ally in Poland — to declare war on Russia. The western Powers delayed their declaration of war on Austria-Hungary until 12 August, by which time the French fleet had finished ferrying troops to France from North Africa and could turn its attention to warfare in the Mediterranean.

1 R.J. **Kerner,** 'The mission of Liman von Sanders. Part IV: the aftermath', *Slavonic and East European Review,* 7, 1928, pp. 90-112.
2 P.W. **Schroeder,** 'World War I as Galloping Gertie: a reply to Joachim Remak', *Journal of Modern History,* xliv, 1972, pp. 319-45.
3 Memorandum by Sektionsrat Franz Baron Matscheko, June 1914, printed in F.R. **Bridge,** *From Sadowa to Sarajevo: the foreign policy of Austria-Hungary, 1866-1914* (London, 1972), pp. 443-48.
4 R.A. **Kann,** *Kaiser Franz Joseph und der Ausbruch des ersten Weltkriegs* (Vienna, 1971).
5 E. **Zechlin,** 'Cabinet versus economic warfare in Germany' in H.W. **Koch** (ed), *The origins of the First World War: German Power and German War Aims* (London, 1972), p. 151 ff.
6 I. **Geiss,** *July 1914: the outbreak of the First World War, selected documents* (London, 1967), pp. 72-4; *Julikrise und Kriegsausbruch 1914* (Hanover 1963), I, no. 24.
7 K.H. **Jarausch,** 'The illusion of a Limited War: Chancellor Bethmann-Hollweg's calculated risk, July 1914', *Central European History,* 2, 1969, p. 58.
8 **Geiss,** *Julikrise,* II, no. 793.
9 F.R. **Bridge,** 'The British declaration of war on Austria-Hungary in 1914', *Slavonic and East European Review,* 47, 1969, pp. 401-22.
10 F.R. **Bridge,** 'Tarde venientibus ossa: Austro-Hungarian colonial aspirations in Asia Minor, 1913-14', *Middle Eastern Studies,* October 1970, pp. 319-30.
11 B.F. **Schulte,** *Vor dem Kriegsausbruch 1914: Deutschland, die Türkei und der Balkan* (Düsseldorf, 1980), p. 93.
12 P.G. **Halpern,** *The Mediterranean Naval Situation 1908-14* (Cambridge, Mass., 1971).
13 **Schulte,** *Kriegsausbruch,* pp. 90-1.
14 J. **Joll,** '1914: the Unspoken Assumptions' in Koch (ed), *Origins,* pp. 307-28.
15 E. **Zechlin,** 'Zwischen Kabinettskrieg und Wirtschaftskrieg', *Historische Zeitschrift,* 199, 1964, p. 400.
16 On these matters see: H.U. **Wehler,** *Das deutsche Kaiserreich 1871-1918* (Göttingen, 1973); the essays in M. **Stürmer** (ed), *Das kaiserliche Deutschland* (Düsseldorf, 1970), particularly H.U. **Wehler,** 'Bismarcks Imperialismus und späte Russlandpolitik unter dem Primat der Innenpolitik' (now available in an English version, H.U. **Wehler,** *The German Empire 1871-1918,* Leamington Spa, 1985); J.G. **Röhl,** *Germany without Bismarck: the crisis of government in the Second Reich 1890-1900* (London, 1967); H.A. **Turner,** 'Bismarck's Imperialist Venture: anti-British in Origin?' in P. **Gifford** and W.R. **Louis** (eds), *Britain and Germany in Africa* (New Haven, Conn., 1967), pp. 47-82.
17 F. **Fischer,** *War of Illusions: German policies from 1911 to 1914* (London, 1975), pp. 362-69.
18 P.M. **Boujou** and H. **Dubois,** *La Troisième République* (Paris, 1963).
19 L. **Albertini,** *The Origins of the War* (London, 1958), II, chapter 13.

Further Reading

On the state of Europe generally in the generation before the First World War see J. Joll, *Europe since 1870: an International History* (Penguin, 1980), and Norman Stone's shorter but brilliant survey, *Europe Transformed, 1878-1919* (Fontana History of Europe, 1983). On the general diplomatic background in the last decades of peace, the student may consult F.R. Bridge and Roger Bullen, *The Great Powers and the European States System, 1815-1914* (London, 1980), before proceeding to A.J.P. Taylor's more complex *The Struggle for Mastery in Europe, 1848-1918* (Oxford, 1951, latest edition 1979), which is still unrivalled in the field. On the developing crisis after about 1911, Richard Langhorne, *The Breakdown of the Concert of Europe* (London, 1981) is a good summary, whereas G. Barraclough's *From Agadir to Armageddon: anatomy of a crisis* (London, 1982) will give readers in the 1980s much food for thought — perhaps, indeed, for concern.

On the whole subject of the origins of the war, the most recent — and unquestionably the best — study, both for the general reader and the student, is J. Joll, *The Origins of the First World War* (London, 1983).

The present state of the debate over war guilt is best summarised in J. Joll, 'The 1914 debate continues: Fritz Fischer and his critics' in H.W. Koch (ed), *The Origins of the First World War: German Power and German War Aims* (London, 1972), pp. 13-29; and the same author's 'War Guilt 1914: a continuing controversy' in *Publications of the German Historical Institute*, IV, 1978, pp. 60-80. Contrasting arguments are developed in more detail in B.E. Schmitt, *The Coming of the War, 1914* (London/New York, 1930), H.E. Barnes, *The Genesis of the World War: an Introduction to the Problem of War Guilt* (New York, 1927) — very pro-German, and S.B. Fay, *The Origins of the World War* (New York, 1928).

P. Kennedy (ed), *The War plans of the Great Powers 1880-1914* (London, 1979) is excellent on military and strategic issues.

On the roles of individual countries the student may consult the relevant volumes in the series 'Foreign Policies of the Great Powers' (Routledge and Kegan Paul), F.R. Bridge, *From Sadowa to Sarajevo: the foreign policy of Austria-Hungary, 1866-1914* (1972); C.J. Lowe and M.L. Dockrill, *The Mirage of Power: British Foreign Policy 1902-1922* (1972); C.J. Lowe and F. Marzari, *Italian Foreign Policy, 1870-1940* (1975), I. Geiss, *German Foreign Policy, 1871-1914* (1976); and I.H. Nish, *Japanese Foreign Policy, 1869-1942* (1977).

On German policy generally, V.R. Berghahn's *Germany and the Approach of War in 1914* is essential reading. A good deal of material has now appeared on the threat to the position of the Central Powers in the Near East and its consequences for Germany's foreign and military policies in the last years of Peace. Fritz Fischer's monumental studies still lead the field: *War of Illusions: German policies from 1911 to 1914* (London, 1975), and *Germany's Aims in the First World War* (London, 1967). Directly relevant to the crisis in the Near East are R.J. Crampton, *The Hollow Detente: Anglo-German relations in the Balkans, 1911-1914* (London, 1980); Fritz Fischer, 'World Policy, World Power and German War Aims', in Koch (ed), *Origins (vide supra)*, and B.F. Schulte, *Vor dem Kriegsausbruch 1914: Deutschland, die Türkei und der Balkan* (Düsseldorf, 1980). On Anglo-German relations, P.M. Kennedy, *The Rise of the Anglo-German Antagonism 1860-1914* (London, 1980) is essential.

The best short account of British policy is Zara S. Steiner, *Britain and the Origins of the First World War* (London, 1977); K.S. Robbins, *Sir Edward Grey* (London, 1971) is lucid and balanced, and F.H. Hinsley (ed), *The Foreign Policy of Sir Edward Grey* (Cambridge, 1977) is a veritable mine of information. K.M. Wilson's *The Policy of the Entente* (Cambridge, 1985) is thought-provoking and for the cabinet's policy in the final crisis, essential.

As regards Russia, the best account for the

student's purposes is D.C.B. Lieven's excellent, balanced, survey, *Russia and the Origins of the First World War* (London, 1983), but important aspects are covered in Dietrich Geyer's majestically detailed *Russian Imperialism: the interaction of domestic and foreign policy, 1860-1914* (Leamington Spa, 1987), L.C.F. Turner, *Origins of the First World War*, I.V. Buestuzhev, 'Russian foreign policy: February-June 1914', *Journal of Contemporary History*, I, 1966, pp. 93-112, and E. Zechlin, 'Graf Witte, Rasputin, and Grossfürst Nikolai Nikolajewitsch', *Krieg und Kriegsrisiko* (Düsseldorf, 1979). On France, the clearest and most manageable account is J.F.V. Keiger, *France and the Origins of the First World War* (London, 1983), but G. Krumeich, *Armaments and Politics in France on the eve of the First World War* (Leamington Spa, 1984) is illuminating in the light of similar studies of Germany. On Austria-Hungary, L. Lafore, *The Long Fuse: an interpretation of the Origins of World War I*

(London, 1966) is a useful introduction to the international implications of the South Slav question; V. Dedijer, *The Road to Sarajevo* (London/New York, 1966) states the Yugoslav case; while N. Stone, 'Hungary and the crisis of July 1914', *Journal of Contemporary History*, 1, 1966, pp. 153-70, and F.R. Bridge, 'The British declaration of war on Austria-Hungary in 1914', *Slavonic and East European Review*, 47, 1969, pp. 401-22 deal with the immediate origins of the war.

On the July crisis generally, see B.E. Schmitt, 'July 1914: Thirty Years After', *Journal of Modern History*, XVI, 1944, pp. 169-204; I. Geiss, *Julikrise und Kriegsausbruch 1914* (2 vols, Hanover, 1963), or the shorter English version, *July 1914: the outbreak of the First World War, selected documents* (London, 1967). The most detailed account is of course still, L. Albertini, *The Origins of the War* (London, 1958), Volumes II and III.